Boydell

The Passion of our Saviour

Boydell

The Passion of our Saviour

ISBN/EAN: 9783742842251

Manufactured in Europe, USA, Canada, Australia, Japa

Cover: Foto ©ninafisch / pixelio.de

Manufactured and distributed by brebook publishing software (www.brebook.com)

Boydell

The Passion of our Saviour

Painted by Carlo Dolce Engraved by R. Earlom

SALVATOR MUNDI

Published March 25, 1809, by Boydell & Co.

Page 13.

Page 23.

Page 44.

Page 62.

Page 126.

Page 139.

Page 205.

Page 284.

www.ingramcontent.com/pod-product-compliance
Lightning Source LLC
Chambersburg PA
CBHW031409160426
43196CB00007B/957